ALMIGHTY GOD CREATOR

ALMIGHTY GOD CREATOR

The Christian Church, Spiritual Law, God's Providential Care, and Odes

B. WHITWORTH-ROOME

VANTAGE PRESS
New York / Los Angeles

FIRST EDITION

Published by Vantage Press, Inc.
516 West 34th Street, New York, New York 10001

Manufactured in the United States of America
ISBN: 0-533-08512-8

Library of Congress Catalog Card No.: 89-90134

To the tremendous power and scope
of God's providence
and to spiritual strength
and godly experience

Contents

Preface

The author as a young man was determined to do something positive in his life! Serious-minded, he turned to religion and a firm belief in God. Providential care and God's love for everything created suggest responsibility as a key to ensure that every individual participates. The intelligent must therefore help the weak as a duty! Providence must have a presence in all the world religions to obtain universality! This objective has great possibilities!

ALMIGHTY GOD CREATOR

One

The Christian Church

Considerations of the present time for thought and prayer.

The Methodist Church

The Methodist church brought into existence by the Wesleys has provided an organization with a personal level of responsibility, "the priesthood of all believers," in line with what we understand by Christ's teaching, as we remember the interval of some fifty years before the early Christians made records and according to discoveries of records up to the present day. In its general setup, it is different from the Anglican church. One claim, made for this change is that it has features providing for differences which reach into the particular feelings of the so-called working class. Furthermore, it has been suggested that it was instrumental, by causing a revulsion of feeling, in stopping the French Revolution from crossing the English Channel.

The Free Churches

The free churches generally have differences from the Anglicans which are well established; in one case they provide for autonomy of congregations under the guidance of a minister.

There is an urgent necessity for an increase in tolerance which will provide and support proper relations in and between all denominations of the Christian church.

Christ, Son of God

Christ's mission to this earth is under the ordinance of God our Father. His mission is generally accepted and while the earth remains, this principal ordinance will be active, setting standards for human conduct under the Christian ethic.

God Almighty

Under God's ordinance no two people are exactly alike. This highlights the necessity for a sound establishment of tolerance.

Down the ages persecution was perpetrated principally against differences in belief in physical things in religious practise. This has been adversely affected, being accentuated and perpetuated by dogma. This still persists in more subtle form. Dogmatism has always been anti-tolerance and as such is a brake on progress. Dogma has seasons during which it increases; we appear to be in one now. Tolerance of differences in belief can only be held and practiced when the wisdom of all God's ordinance is understood, especially his creation of differences in human characteristics; yet, when looked at from a right angle, the latter becomes obvious, for one can clearly see how flat life would be if we were created all alike. Perhaps it is in prayer that we have the best opportunity of fully appreciating the necessity for, and quality of, tolerance on the firm basis of reason.

Spiritual Law

We must proceed to a firm belief that a positive advance in knowledge of the spiritual laws of the universe is the greatest need of the age.

Perhaps we have erred in thinking of these laws as the Holy Ghost. We must reflect on our situation when we leave this earth dependent upon them. Nothing physical will then avail us. Our fortitude will be our soul.

God's Providence

Thinking of man's continuance as a rational being, there is a pressing need for him to discard as unproductive his use of force in inhuman violence. Here there is, as plain as can be, a directive in God's Providence, as exemplified by Christ. The spiritual laws must also convince man with a sure corrective, away from his acquisitive actions, in the use of force in war. The rectitude of man's demands must be the criterion, and in that day there will be funds available for many worthwhile projects; readily at hand will be the released human energy to carry them into effect.

Obligations Arising out of Intelligence

This is not idealism gone mad. It's a suggestion that the time has arrived when we must put our intelligence to a test by showing an ability to think in some depth upon the problems which confront us. It must be said that such a major step forward will probably have to await world government, but time is pressing, and when the time is ripe, the abandonment of force will require political action. The church at that time must be first in the field, advocating an unswerving conviction that spiritual power only can bring about a major change of heart, which will be permanent. The psychological moment, this opportunity, must not be lost, for who is to say how devastating that would prove to be? Atomic energy is the great danger. It has the potential to destroy our civilization, or shall I say, to stop our progress into a vision of a more soundly based civilization, the grounds for which have still to be worked out, needing all our energies.

Spiritual Law

Regarding spiritual law, the universe is under the rule of moral laws. Christian belief is in accord, and it is deduced from the complete reliance which can be placed upon the observable and calculable nature of the physical laws, which are in operation. The control of these laws, after establishment, could not be of a physical nature because of the distances involved; therefore, it is logical to look at the possibilities. The experiences of life, especially those with a psychological basis, point to the existence of a law which in operation is equal in reliability to the physical law. This law operates upon conscious processes of the mind, a stage in human experience which is spiritual; it secures progress in development.

For instance, there is the longterm nature of Providence, the evolution which provides for the security and continuance of life on earth, as was the case early in the twentieth century when the evolution of synthetic fertilizers made possible an increased production of food, necessary because of increasing world population. Providence, in hand with evolution, has occasioned a multitude of instances wherein the chemist and others have evolved ways of supplementing nature in this way, so saving a very adverse situation from arising.

There is an equal evolution upon which processes, enhancing and making progressive spiritually, conscious activity of the mind; in acceptance and belief in providence, have effectively increased mental activity in research, making advances of note. In a mundane situation, and after a struggle, the abolition of slavery was brought about in a struggle, the abolition of slavery was brought about in a similar way, which in the future will abolish blackmail and the violence occasioned by it. The great waste and the mental strife in families will be eliminated also, when negotiation is established as the rule—a real step forward, because negotiation can and will be administered on a positive basis.

There are many human problems which await this spiritual development, which will no doubt bring into consideration the economics of each situation being negotiated, as a matter important to all parties concerned. We will hope that as a direct result of this and the attention it receives, it will be seen to have a superiority over present practice, and when fully appreciated, it will gain momentum.

The Human Conscience

A very important matter in this spiritual advancement into experience of human possibilities is its effect on the human conscience. This character-forming component of the human mind has a great potential as a progressive influence throughout life, full and free, and of an advancing, developing nature. This development is under the influence of very many observations and should be a feature in education, much more positive than it is at present. The teacher can increase the effectiveness of every subject in the curriculum, but in the modern school, with noise out of control and discipline slack, there is much hindrance.

However, too much importance can be given to years at school, for this is a lifelong development. As such it should be marked by special application, including features which will inculcate a knowledge of the existence of mental processes of an ever-expanding and increasing nature, opening up new avenues to mental ability, which will outstrip present knowledge and provide technique capable of exploring the spiritual component of personality. This is important because it will secure new ability to take advantage psychologically of the increasing possibilities which will be required to deal with the problems of the world of the future and be alongside the tremendous advances in physics and medical science, for example, which are ahead in development.

This points to the urgent necessity to restore the balance by promoting exploration of spiritual law, so as to bring about improvements in human behaviour and so to push the brute into the background and thus have continuous consideration by each and every individual who can be contacted. The advent of a new concept of the influence of spiritual law upon human affairs can be seen as a great step forward, as was the giant step forward by the advent of Christ, after the providential preparation of the world for his coming by the Jews of some three to four thousand years ago.

Stages of Evolution

Stages of evolution, as seen through the light of history, provide a very productive study, as they beam enlightenment under the Providence of the great Creator and Provider, the Almighty God. There is a constant feature in providence: everything evolved comes under the common factor of longterm love. Christ sowed a great and wonderful seed when he said "God is a spirit, and they that worship him must worship him in spirit and in truth."

The Fruits of the Spirit

A spiritual concept of great moment is wisdom. It is an attainment, not a gift, and must always be actively the subject of progressive advancement and development, for there is no apex in any branch of knowledge. The fruits of the spirit, its components, are: Love, the premier, and out of love come sensitiveness, sympathy, mercy, understanding, and tolerance. The Christian ethic, based on love, has faith and hope as cardinal virtues. Also deduced and/or implied by the spirit thereof are principle, conviction, idealism, and consideration. Character, when developed on the Christian ethic, is a combination of these in practice, along with Christian virtues, such as fellowship, sublimity, unselfish service, and satisfaction, arising out of continuous and very active endeavour; it is a developing virtue of increasing experience. It is thus an advancing attainment. All are based and activated by love.

Sacrifice Central in Christianity

These qualities have their foundation in spiritual law, and at their heart is the central theme of Christianity, sacrifice, a theorem for every individual Christian, very personal as exemplified by Christ. Always in deep feeling when we experience a desire to increase our knowledge of the ethereal nature of God's love. In its perfect animative power is to impart life, and as we experience the feelings arising from the sure knowledge that his love is universal, given without discrimination, with a nature which is absolute, then we are in the most lofty and exalted walks of life, a realm quite distinct from mere existence. Smitten by thoughts of our obligations and the demands we must live up to, consoled by our belief that strength to meet our tasks is promised, we resolve that we will strive mightily and not be found wanting.

Christian Duty

The Christian of experience has a clear duty; to show concern by acting decisively in adding their experience, with all the influence they can exert, upon the spread of knowledge of the Christian ethic, beyond the circle of their friends, spending little time on things of lesser value, devoting time and thought on the development of belief and understanding of the spiritual laws of the universe. A daunting task of our age!

Inherent Difficulty

On the subject of the current craze for organic union of sections of the Christian Church, which arose because of taunting by observers of disagreement between them, started along with the modern trust which is placed in large concerns. This has its origin in the hierarchy, not in the churches. The move in this direction in industry and commerce is now deplored by many as they view the actions of multinational companies. These concerns become very impersonal, and they operate avoiding the control exercised through company law. This can be done because this legislation is national.

In the case of religion, surely the emphasis must be placed on a very personal and individual level, to be in line with Christ. Cardinal virtue is in fact a very personal element intrinsic and individual in religion, requiring worship and obedience to God. The Christian has to stand up to adversity of many kinds, rising above it, being good tempered when confronted, openly admitting imperfection, and pointing out the ordinances of God, who created all people different one from another, as a very good reason for exercising deep thought upon creation.

Problems in Evolution

The reason behind these created differences is not hard to work out. The advances that have been made, though slowly—as is always the case in evolution, where a small step forward takes what we regard as a long time—are a direct result of different approaches to problems, leading to successful outcomes. Allowing for consolidation before embarking on change shows wisdom and understanding of a high order and avoids making a change without these virtues being brought into play.

There is much evidence of change for the sake of change alone. This can also be described as crazed. It can cause much unhappiness and dissatisfaction; it can often be seen in a distracted facial expression and can bring about withdrawal and result in a wasted life. There has been down the ages, as a study of history will show, much loss of ability which could have been applied, but for precipitate action, which has disrupted purposeful progressive action, the essential personal element being outsted. Intrinsic virtue is able to stand alone and should not be thrown into outer darkness with loss of zeal. The Christian virtues of consideration and the like are not being overworked.

There is much which is enigmatic in the present call for change. It can be called inconsiderate and nonsensical in view of Christ's life so close to his teaching. There are many urgent matters, touched upon here, especially in the churches, which are being neglected. Energy is being wrongly applied. One most important consideration, which cannot be too strongly stressed, is the effect which would be a direct result of a too-hurried attempt to bring about union of sections of the Christian Church. This is the disagreement of many, who have made it plain that in the event they would secede. There are a large number who would go with the tide and thereafter be mere ciphers.

There is present already, in Methodism, a legacy from what has proved to be a mistaken union of the Wesleyans, Primitives, and United Methodists, which took place in the thirties. Almost at once there were church closures. There was dissatisfaction, especially amongst ministers, as the strong overcame the weak without showing any proper feeling, consideration being conspicuous by its absence on too many occasions. Loss of members resulted and coverage decreased.

The writer has for more than half a century lived in several parts of England, the Northeast, the Northwest, Midlands, the Southwest, and in Scotland, east and west, preached in hundreds of churches and held high office. Not once, in his hearing, was the subject of union with another denomination mentioned in any church.

I finish with a few Parthian shots.

Saint Paul said:

> His work was in demonstration of the spirit and of power.
>
> Your faith should not stand in the wisdom of men but in the power of God.
>
> —1 Corinthians 2:4–5

> Has thou faith? Have it to thyself before God.
>
> Happy is he that condemneth not himself in that thing which he alloweth!
>
> —Romans 14:22

Saint Paul's wisdom must be decisive. Not by words alone but by their acts shall they be established and become the disciples of their Master.

What is looked for here is participation by many in serious consideration of all things worthwhile, especially the spiritual element in religion.

Forward!

Two

The Further Development of Knowledge of the Spiritual Laws of the Universe

The World Situation

Conflict is increasing all over the world. Easy communication is requiring a standard of human conduct and relations difficult to establish on an international basis.

Man is capable of intelligent understanding, and it appears that in this he is at present being severely tested; no small effort will be sufficient to justify him. It is necessary for him to examine his obligations and responsibilities.

History and accomplishments on record, along with sociology, religion, and philosophy, require to be studied at some depth. Man is very much inclined to take things for granted.

There is now the need for a fresh look at past, present, and future. No time should be lost; action is imperative, but the times are now different and no longer is it possible for one man to solve the problems which face us, as it was in the past. Neither will precipitate action meet the present need.

The necessity is to be discursive because of the very different lights in which fundamentals can be seen to need establishing on the spiritual plane. Therefore, what would seem at first glance to be repetition must be tolerated in order to reach a proper conclusion.

Many things on the physical plane have a not-so-obvious function in that it is a demonstration platform, which indicates the necessity to examine the possibility of moving forward into other and important fields. A Prerequisite is a study of the individual human and the fact that there are no two created alike. Also in evolution, as history plainly shows, long years are required to prepare the ground for each step forward. The precise nature and degree of each step—also the implications and all aspects—as the future is envisaged, are measures being revealed as to further development, remembering that there is no apex to be achieved here on Earth! This can be expressed as establishing stages in progress from which to further develop. The time is ripe to move forward in understanding arising from the ordinances of the Creator of the Universe, the Author of Providence, the central control in creation, not yet fully recognized or taken into account in advanced religious circles.

The Command of Christ

The command of Christ, the Son of God, was to worship God, his Father, the spirit of creation in the universe, in spirit and in truth. There can be no greater concept, and man can only neglect that command with compunction and to his ultimate extinction.

The whole course of life on Earth could be altered would man but see the necessity to bring all his thinking upon religion, his actions, and relationships into line with what he can observe of the spirit of God in creation and Providence. The spirit of God is providing, for his whole creation, long-term good, as Christ, his Son, saw it, lived by it, and taught it!

The Christian Ethic

The Christian ethic is preeminent in the world as a way of life, from whatever standpoint you view it, with the welfare and good of humanity in mind. There are of course other contributions, but nothing better. Everything worthwhile is progressive, and this will be better understood and appreciated as we increase our knowledge of the universe, of which our Earth is a part. Two thousand years after Christ, who said, "In my Father's house are many mansions," we have an ever-increasing knowledge of the universe as a habitat and can speculate on the state of development of life on planets, which are governed by suns, compared with which our sun is a very small source of energy. This increasing knowledge should help us to see the necessity for the removal of the reasons for many people remaining inactive.

Here is demonstrated one reason why faith is such an important feature of the Christian religion: because distances in the universe are so great that there cannot be any physical connection between our earth and other inhabited planets; only on the spiritual plane can the distances be commuted. There is also a gulf between the undoubted very difficult life which is demanded of the Christian in all aspects, in observance of the Christian ideal, and the carefree selfish life of many people. The object of this thesis is to enlist the help of intellectuals and thoughtful people in establishing an understanding of all the possibilities of saving our civilization, securing a belief in the absolute requirement for progress and development along every available channel, and thus raising the quality of life on earth and securing a future for mankind. This earth can best be seen as a training ground. All training has its difficulties and without them life would be a dead, flat affair. More important, the objects of creation in establishing development as a continuous process would be negatived and lost.

Violence and Blackmail

The signs of our times are marked by a growing sense of disquiet at the way in which violence is spreading under many very active agencies, as rule by law is being disregarded or deliberately set on one side. Standards of conduct generally are being lowered. Responsibility is being discarded! The umpire and the referee are being attacked. The law of legislature is being flouted and thieving is widespread. Blackmail is used to secure unfair proportions. It is openly claimed that a degree of success is being achieved by departing from the requirement of legal assessment.

The foregoing are signs that the current inadequate degree of civilization is losing ground and every human who claims to be compos mentis has a duty to his fellows to be personally concerned in studying the steps required to reverse this trend. Furthermore, these are only some of the signs. There are others less obvious. Were it possible to make a survey, this state of affairs would be found to be the direct result of progressive measures in the human being impeded. Man can only secure his future by directing great effort to an emergence from his present state.

This emergence is to be achieved by increasing his knowledge and understanding of the spiritual law governing progress in his development. This in turn can only be fully appreciated by recognition of the ordinances of the Creator, specifically aimed to overcome and progress beyond the confines of animal instinctive action, advancing by a state of conscious development to a standard of conduct which will empower the human being by a sense of the urgency to make positive efforts to rise out of animal limentation, thus appreciating the objects of divine Providence! To have it (divine Providence) recognized would be a major victory.

The Jews' Great Contribution

The Israelites, a horde of escaping slaves traveling in semi-desert country after bondage in Egypt, were subjected to the setting up of a code of conduct devised by Moses: but they rebelled, feeling a desire to exploit their newfound freedom, and it became imperative in the mind of Abram to break away. This had a direct effect, and Abram's vision led him to leave the slight security of his tribe, and as recorded in the Old Testament, he took with him his relatives and immediate people and went forth to seek a new land of opportunity, away from the despotism and insecurity in which they were floundering. The result was a development far beyond his expectations but very much in line with his hope.

The Jewish nation, which he founded as a direct result, made progress in moving away from the ancient idolators and sun worshipers and established belief in the creative spirit of the universe! This was to lead to the messianic concept. These progressive steps are worth much study because of the spiritual nature of the means by which they were developed, away from physical and mental processes. They moved into a media which has lost ground. Much understanding of spiritual activation, selfless in its practice, can lead to appreciation of the development possibilities designed for and required of the human being under ordinance, the creative authority's objective.

The Concept of Law

The resolution of Abraham was a strong step forward from the falling away, which occurred subsequent to Moses introducing the concept of living under law, the Creator having been credited with forming the world and everything in it, as recorded in Genesis. The dawning of there being a spiritual component in the human's makeup awaiting development could have received strength from whispers heard in Egypt arising out of ancient mysticism, but more positive strength was evidenced in the prophets who had some of the first records of man to encourage their vision, greatly strengthened by a new devotional acknowledgement of the Creator God. This was a marked contribution to progress.

The Advent of Christ

The advent of Christ, with his advanced teaching, so impressed his disciples and apostles that they in turn after his death were determined to impress their hearers and became over enthusiastic in inventing physical miracles to give weight to their very firm belief. Without this early conviction, which has proved successful in its purpose, it being a supplement to certain acts of Christ's, performed out of his knowledge of spiritual law we might not have the fruits today, for who can say that this enlightenment would have persisted? Rather might it have been allowed to evaporate into mythology.

Appreciation, a fundamental component of spiritual strength, took hold and was sufficient to secure for future generations to think upon, as wonders of development and advancement, every single item of Christ's teaching. Furthermore, there was a necessity two thousand years ago to invent a series of supporting events to impress on future generations the absolute importance to the human race of a completely new and far-reaching morality which was being taught fearlessly by one Jesus of Nazareth. The act of recording for the benefit of future generations was in itself a major exercise in that day. This has resulted in delays, which were, however beneficial, because it was necessary to invent events purely to give credence to the fact that in the minds of the people of that era these were events of the greatest importance. They were seen as a great step forward in human progress and had to be securely fixed in the minds of the people of that age as a first step.

Progress demands modifications in many fields of knowledge, for very good reasons. As an example, in the scientific field, one can cite the very acceptable theories which the astronomer Sir James Jeans put forward sixty or so years ago as up-to-date theories of the nature of the universe itself, many of which have since been dealt with by Cambridge University astronomers, Americans, and others in very drastic manner.

Everything worthwhile is continuous in its development. Christ demonstrated this time after time in His dealings with people. His knowledge of the art and science of human relations can be studied with great advantage and practiced with beneficial results. There are rewards for a lifelong involvement in these spiritual developments, which are components of the ordinances of the creative spirit of the universe. Christ said, "God is a spirit, and they that worship him must worship him in spirit and in truth."

Little interest is shown in these words of Christ's as is the case with far too much of His teaching. Many people subscribe to the belief that the Christian ethic, as taught by Christ, is far in advance of any other earthly morality which has been put forward. The church Christ founded fails in many respects to purposefully follow his teaching in ways which will lead to practical service, offered to mankind generally. Too many are content to exist in a closed circuit.

The direct result is a lack of the knowledge and experience which the spiritual laws of the universe are designed to provide. These laws exist in order to secure ever-increasing effectiveness in the divinely inspired direction of development and progress, thus coming into line with the object of divine ordinance. In fact it can be added that this would be in accord with the astronomers' concept of an expanding universe, governed by divine ordinance in universal harmony and demonstrated in the positive nature of what we observe as we look out on the universe from Earth!!

Universal Long-Term Good

The great creative spirit of the universe is a spirit of universal goodwill incomprehensively contracted to a span and made by God the Creator a possible reality in man! Has man grasped this? Does he act upon it? What is the evidence? What percentage pay heed?

Man's ego, his egotism, seems to have tripped him up when he was on the way to understanding that with which the creative spirit would have furnished his mind. It penetrated his conscience to give him a vision of the persistence down the ages of this same spirit, as it moved over the face of this earth to enliven humans to the ordinance present in the scheme of things, inspiring it to develop into individual consciousness. The best of comprehension was demonstrated in the words of Christ when he said, "God is a spirit, and they that worship him must worship him in spirit and in truth."

To come to a full comprehension of the truth, which is ever developing, was part of Christ's mission, as was made clear when he said, "This is life eternal, that they might know Thee the only true God and Jesus Christ whom thou hast sent" (John 17). Further, "When he the spirit of truth is come, he will guide you into all truth" (John 16). Indispensable is the necessity that the individual must develop by faith! Those who fail to appreciate this would condemn humans to a state where they would be as puppets on the end of a controlling cord.

The Physical State

Christianity must progress by turning away from some of the improbable physical items of belief to the real, much more important, spiritual basis. It must make progress in knowledge and understanding of the spiritual laws of the universe because everything of worth in creation is progressive on this basis alone. A proper and generally acceptable theorem is essential because things which are wrongly based are always liable to fly off at a tangent. Lacking a base for progress, they lose out and become meaningless or are inadequate and partial, as is the case at present where "faith healing," which is universal, is being used wrongly.

Claims are being made for faith healing which is supernatural. Mind has long been known to have power over matter, and much can be achieved. Much more is possible if the theorem of spiritual law is accepted and worked upon to give this movement a natural foundation from which to proceed, increasing its power by effective progress, using the patient's mind. Another step forward now being envisaged, perceived by intuition.

Further Progressive Steps

The adherence of the Church with fanatical persistence to the inclusion in belief of departures from physical fact is having more than one brake on progress. The greatest of these is in disregard and neglect in acquiring knowledge of spiritual law. The spiritual laws of the universe are just as real and understandable as the scientific laws and have the same place in maintenance, but they are the greater where progress and development are concerned, because they will illumine the pathway to much-needed progress and understanding of survival after death and transference to take part in a future life: the concept of eternity.

There are so many facets to knowledge, even accepting the limits of the finite mind, that it is reasonable to be convinced that all the indications suggest that this life, in many respects, can be but a beginning. Many concepts are obviously capable of being developed, but only in a future life. One realizes when thinking upon these lines that faith is indispensable in the present scheme of things. It conveys in a spiritual light a conviction of far greater possibilities in the future. We have the existence and extension, as it were, of things comprehended only in part, which, could they be realized, here and now, would cancel out faith, will power, endeavour, and other special qualities. For this reason we are not able to know the future positively.

The more knowledge one acquires, the more it is realized how very little one can know. To put it another way, how little you really know of your own special subject, upon which you have spent much time. Always there is that feeling of greater opportunities in a greater light here and hereafter. Second in importance as a brake on progress is an attempt to stand still or the negligence in standing still, which is wrong. The ordinance under God is a law under which you go forward or slip back from your attainment. It is symptomatic that an attainment must first be maintained and then further developed. Looking at an important detail of Christ's life, the manner and the way in which he dealt with people, you must, if unbiased, recognize a wonderful understanding of psychology superior to anything at present generally practiced in any walk of life.

Human Relationship

There is the immediate necessity to probe to the depths of the psychology of human relationship in order to improve on the present very low measure of success being achieved, by those who practise in negotiations, apparently with less than the degree of understanding required to conduct matters which bear, for example, on relationships in industry, commerce, and employment generally. A more comprehensive knowledge of the elements of the spiritual laws of the universe would ensure urgently needed improvement. Many underhand practices are tolerated, which a greater light on spiritual rectitude would subdue and in time abolish, as humans advance from animal instincts to a more rational working of the enlarging human brain.

To this and the energy of intellectuals who cannot accept certain extreme departures from credibility in a purely physical matter or state, they should be reconciled and brought into active participation. These people who hold aloof are themselves deficient in both knowledge of and belief in the spiritual laws governing the universe. Evolution, operating in the light of revelation and working in the strength of an increased knowledge of spiritual law, gained with the assistance of reconciled intellectuals, could improve on partial concepts too narrow to appreciate the full force of the ordinances of the creative spirit. These can be seen in the vision of the ancient seers in the Old Testament who worked under the influence of revelation, aided by conviction gained from a knowledge of the following: application of logic applied in the sense of right over might, mind over matter, faith, hope, mercy, forgiveness, humanity, moral character, integrity, unselfishness of working for the general good, general experience out of working with people. The list is so long that it is obvious that it simply must be made the intensive study of as many people as can be reached by a media specially designed for such a purpose, strong enough to resist the cold water thrown upon something new by reactionaries, because the magnanimous creator has a task for every member of his creation.

It should be noted that all have been endowed as individuals in his sight; further, that all have a personal contribution which the creater looks to each to make. Their failure means that their piece of work goes forever undone, involving that individual in a responsibility under circumstances which are complex. However, this should be understood by all intelligent people working under the aegis of the Christian ethic; others could be exonerated.

Christ's Disciples

Christ spent much time preparing his disciples for the time when he would leave them, in order that they would be capable to teach with clarity the loving Providence of his Father. This should indicate and make abundantly clear to every Christian the absolute nature of what he expects of each of them, which is a personal commitment to strive with might and main to follow in His steps.

Development of the Human

The spiritual laws of the universe, still far from being fully understood, are the Creator's ordinance for development of the human. They are necessary to supplement mentality and are man's only way of developing beyond and away from the condition which governs the animal in its limitation!

Hindrance to Progress

There is one hindrance to progress which a greater understanding of spiritual law would eliminate. That is the petty jealousy between and within the different sections of the Christian Church. More important, there are many practices in the form of persecution, which have been present down the ages and which have found support amongst dignitaries of the church. These disgraceful acts—attempts to hold up progress—would likewise be eliminated in a greater spiritual light, because it would be seen that to be corrupted by power is a great and damaging weakness. There must follow a greater consciousness of accountability, and it is suggested that this could only be brought about under the light of spiritual revelation, only available to individuals sensitive to divine ordinance. There would always be the high probability that it would also be the means of enlightenment which would reduce evil in the world.

The Survival of Mankind

Man's survival is dependent upon spiritual development and progress to widespread conscious accountability, most urgently necessary because of the spreading to all nations capable of using it, the know-how of the manufacture and uses of atomic power. A set of circumstances can be envisaged where, by a series of mistakes, atomic missiles could be fired. The early warning system could then retaliate and be the direct cause of a holocaust. The evils of this proliferation make this an eventuality which can only be prevented by a great upsurge of conviction which will have the power and the will to establish a degree of far-seeing wisdom, grasping clearly a responsibility to control and then destroy the atomic weapons, alter the conditions which warranted their manufacture, and further proceed to eliminate many developments of evil potential now facing the nations, threatening disruption and widespread destruction.

There is only one source for the development of this far-seeing wisdom which is available to mankind, and that is in the ordinances of the Creater God of this universe—divine Providence producing a spiritual understanding, an eventual safeguard, the premise for building a structure in essence spiritual, which will secure the future, being powered by the element of ineffable love!

Scientists, out of their observations and knowledge of the universe claim to have evidence of exploding stars. There is some ground to support a theory that this could result from chain reactions set up by atomic explosions!

Surely it is not only the safety of mankind that is at stake! If the question was asked: What is the object of life? Or, why are we created? What is the purpose of our existence? Because we are created different from one another, the answers would vary a very wide range, except for the statement, "I haven't ever given it a thought," or, "I have not thought of the reason for my existence seriously."

The Reasons for Existence (Not Exhaustive)

We seldom take serious notice of what is said by people who talk about the universe, the evidence of which is the stars in the sky. We are always interested in pictures thereof!

One reason for this is that our minds are finite. They are bound by limit as opposed to infinite—having no bounds or limits, endless, greater than any assignable quantity.

We have many things to occupy us and when we have a special interest, we are not able to spend more than a limited amount of time upon it, even when we are professional. We have a body and a brain. We have intelligence, which can illumine our interests. The variety of our interests is inexhaustible, but developing them is limited by opportunity, time, and cost in energy and money. However, we have freedom of choice. We can decide and determine, be selfish or otherwise. We can concentrate or proliferate. The treatise you have read gives a very important affirmation to what I believe is most important in this life. It is solemn, serious, and absorbing. Nothing I have writen is as important to you as your own thought on the subject.

My whole purpose is to stimulate your thought and secure your contribution. I cannot, of course, demand it or influence it against your will.

I would, therefore, say the reasons for our existence are inexhaustive and of prime importance to every individual. I would liken the detail of them to the number of stars in the sky.

THREE

Detail of Major Items of God's Providence and Its Objectives

In order of Creation: first, *God's Providence*, the provision in the universe of huge envelope of gas from which our solar system was evolved.

Second in order of importance: The outstanding achievement of the Jewish nation in establishing belief in an *Almighty Creator* and the teaching of Christ, the Son of God! He highlights all the wonderful love in the universe! God's love!

The Christian ethic began to be in evidence in Christ's lifetime because of the contacts he made with people in his day. It continues to reflect all that is best in man's thinking! The Christian Church has faithfully followed Christ's instruction to go into all the world to preach salvation. Let us remember that the spiritual development which Christ teaches is a requirement to fit us for participation; it is at such moments that we experience a glimpse of spiritual fulfilment! The recording of Christ's life and teaching began fifty years after his death!

During the last two thousand years, progressive thinking has almost been rejected. Resourceful minds of Lutheran quality have achieved Reformation. The Augsburg Confession gives us a piece of advanced thinking. The Church has persecuted whenever disbelief even in material things, has come to the knowledge of people in authority, some of whom were known to be wrongdoers, deserving punishment.

Justice, so called, is prodigal, very often seen to being wrongly administered, with those in office unfit to govern. Complacency must be a most rare feeling, almost absent from alert minds, in view of tendencies in the world at large today! Thoughtful love was projected into the massive provision in the universe. Aeons in advance of the creation of mankind, for whom it was preparing, this refers to our Earth.

In God's hands the sun, a great basic atomic power, came into being, the source from which our solar system was evolved! There are greater sources of energy in the universe.

We now concentrate upon our Earth!

It is set at the required distance from the sun (93 million miles) to suport LIFE! The surface temperature of the sun is 12,000 degrees Fahrenheit. The Earth's distance is calculated. If it were miles nearer to the sun, we would be roasted; if miles farther away, frozen. The other planets are not in position to support life. The following details are exact: the Earth rotates on its axis one thousand miles an hour to control our length of day. Further calculation ensures that the Sun's power is correctly distributed.

The Earth is tilted at an angle of 23 degrees on its axis, to give us our seasons as it journeys round the sun. The thickness of the Earth's crust is right so that oxygen can be evolved to support life. The density of the atmosphere is right, or some of the millions of meteors that burn in the atmosphere would burn up the Earth's surface.

The depth of the ocean is set to support vegetable life. The moon is distanced to control the tides. Its average distance from Earth is 238,840 miles. If both maximum and minimum were reduced by, say, twenty-thousand miles, so bringing it nearer, a good deal of the Earth's surface would be flooded twice a day, causing great destruction. Even the mountains would be eroded away. There can be no variation, for all features are calculated exactly at what is required to fit in to the grand design of Providence!

The items of Providence which are quoted are examples; very many more can be referred to. All are calculated and are without variation. There is abundant evidence in Providence, which is one hundred percent practical; not one single thing in creation is an accident! On the contrary everything is by intelligent design, using our known, established mathematical law by which the wonderful exactness of God's creation is formulated!

In our solar system, the powerful preponderance of the beneficial, as the true spirit of providential care for the individual, is in evidence. God, the very spirit of Creation for the eventual benefit of the human being, does so without discrimination of the slightest degree. For instance, the fruits of the Earth are for the whole of creation, and they come into existence under the greatest force in the universe: the pure love of its Creator. Man interferes, but that is *not* being considered under *this* exercise.

The whole of Creation is under the great spiritual law of the universe. This control is in clear evidence, as we look out from Earth. It is not fully understood. We do not know from where in the universe it is operated or maintained, but we see its perfect order! We can be sure that God has created it, and so we have good reason to believe that it is one of the foundations upon which our faith can rest!

That faith holds a great belief in a life after this life. It has a surety because of conviction arising out of many revelations firmly held because of many and various spiritual experiences, begun here on Earth, will be brought to fruition in a greater light! We can enter into a further understanding, evolving naturally as an obvious continuance under spiritual law, to be illuminated in the hereafter. This can be seen as an illustration of the ultimate power there is in faith to reveal practical results, when it is firmly held! Thinking about the future points unmistakably to the Majesty of God; a great reality, capable of using an intelligence which we can observe, has accomplished a great achievement in the orderly universe.

We see the scope as we see in Providence how each individual component is exactly right for the duty which it is designed to perform, in correct relation with all components. This is in design, function, dimension, position, strength, physical properties, etc. A loving regard for all things created is very desirous and must not be overlooked. We must have an ever increasing awareness of God in our life here on Earth. It will then become a natural progression to see clearly that which Christ emphasized when talking of his Father and the eternal life which his Father actually lives and offers to his children!

Providence, as provided in the universe, must be studied and made known; it needs to be well understood and acknowledged. This is an urgent necessity, it being a basic reason for the question asked in this exercise! Millions more of the people on Earth must be influenced by these wonders of Creation! Conduct must be revolutionized. Knowledge of quality must be raised to a distinguishing character held with pride by teeming millions of resolute people, thus correcting the downward trend of this age and producing solid advancement. Things that mitigate our knowledge of spiritual life must be brought out into the open!

Two major items of creation which are providential are the tides and the laving of the Earth by the rain. Tremendous energy is employed, quite beyond man's ability to provide! The tides keep the Earth sweet, and the rain does a large number of essential operations, growth being the chief of these. Triumph! Of God's Providence!

The Scriptures (written by men) inspired by God and through Christ are basic to the question asked herein.

The Christian ethic arose from the scriptures, they being the only record of the teaching of Christ. It is by far superior to all the world's religions. It is a great need which is being neglected for lesser activity, which makes it imperative that we also have an exact knowledge of Providence, so that in it we can be sure we are close to an awareness of God as Creator using the great spiritual power of creative love. Such intelligence is foundation on which to hold to our faith in God.

Hundreds of thousands of people who have no religion could be influenced by the subjective nature of Creation. It is part of a long life of plentiful experience when thinking and speaking with devotees to touch upon spiritual realities. Confidence is mutual and that atmosphere makes for a special open-mindedness with charitable overtones. Love is in evidence and opportunity can be grasped. There is a movement into speculative freedom, and immediate thinking deepens into lovely uplifting expression; there follows an urge to achieve! It is at such moments of spiritual expression with our devotees that we sense being on the verge of insight into a development of new and revealing spiritual awareness of God in a breathtaking light!

A greater knowledge of Providence in much detail would turn people away from some of the evils of the day!

Too many people nowadays indulge in wrongdoing, lacking the ability to reject the permissiveness which is overtaking our age! They are not aware of the character-forming influence of discipline and therefore do not experience the need for sacrifice in their life. Other features of the Christian ethic also are outside of their life's experience. Falling and failing standards are not seen as destructive of principles. They turn away, failing to recognize the edifice of principles which require their particular support as conscious individuals, thus denying their status. Mawkish activity is preferred, and a lower mentality is the result!

Are we giving enough thought to the increasing portion of time which is being given to acquisitiveness of material possessions? Could we be accused of breeding battalions of cyphers, people giving up much of intrinsic value for things of lesser value—money, for instance? Will this drift land us into a position from which we will be unable to adjust, locked fast in desperate error?

Falling standards suggest we are stopping short; giving insufficient consideration.

Gloom which subjected to a cheerful reception will back down; it is very deceptive and will easily take you in, causing you to mistake it for ordinary thinking! You are then startled to realize it is most serious and in fact, right outside your control! The incidence of this sad state is on the increase, both in intensity and number of occurrences. How to deal with it proves, at sight, to require special powers. You find you require help, and in most cases it is available from a friend or adviser.

In all of this, we have just touched the fringe of the possibilities. We can turn to lesser things to occupy our minds or, on individual right, stay on the subject and seek further progressive thought to furnish our minds and hearts, thus satisfying our best instincts.

The Creator's Providential Care

Since the beginning of time, and still operational in the universe in our time, there is a God-created ordinance which bears equally on every living organism. It is the Almighty Creator's Universal Providential Care. Only a small percentage of people realize its existence, living under its benefits with acknowledgement and undertstanding. This ordinance is in vogue throughout creation; it surrounds the human and the animal on Earth. The human intimately at the elbow lifelong, with a plethora of beneficial effects upon our wonderfully designed bodies and capable minds. The animal, prompted by instinct, has full advantage of Providence, which is therefore one hundred percent effective. All this is appreciated by humans who have an active mind and a conscience, the human very largely in a state of uninterest, being without vital knowledge! It is intended to make this abundantly plain by the detailing of items of God's care in Providence. See the whole of this!

Millions of people in all the world's religions could be attracted and influenced towards participating, by being informed of the details of God's Providence. It is no secret! There is an opportunity to return thanks! The problem is to turn people away from many of thir negative and unrewarding pursuits towards a knowledge of the intrinsic quality of every item of providential care, many of which they are unwittingly enjoying because there are so many of them in operation and readily available. A principal objective for all of us is to secure a substantial mental attainment to enable us thereby to give a service to our day and generation, by learning the details of Providential care and then demonstrating our knowledge, explaining its impact clearly! The human has the power of reason and therefore can appreciate man's limitations. Man could not provide the enormous amount of energy which nature employs in providing these very numerous conditions and services, which make life on Earth bearable.

Most of the people referred to believe in God the Creator of the universe and would profit by this knowledge. There is a great need at present for all people to be concerned in bringing these facts into the open. Future efforts towards progress and improvement depend upon massive support from people conversant with present destructive tendencies, having the will to act energetically, unequivocally, to reverse them! This cannot be overstressed. There is in it a great personal responsibility, the need for people to come to this knowledge and take action upon it!

Tremendous improvements in many directions discovered

and helped into usefulness by man's imagination and ingenuity will grind to a halt unless mental alertness springs into action. At present thousands of interdependent requirements demand adjustment; exact recognition and positive corrective action are essential to secure drastic alteration and so revert to a much more stable and reasonable state. The present day is faced with the lowering and destruction of standards of conduct. There is no understanding of such a happening in the presence of providential care.

An individual, by careful observation, can come to understand many interesting things in nature, which will illumine the mind and inform on items of providential care. There are very many known items of Providence in addition to those named herein, many of which are relative to individual acts, which happen without being recognized as providential. Trial-and-error events, by accident, experiments aiming hopefully at one result and chancing upon another, all within Providence.

Man cannot germinate seed; he can prepare it, under Providence, for germination by the Sun. Many thousands of years ago, he saw green vegetation for the first time; it was primitive stuff, and after a time he saw it was growing.

Man started primitive farming thousands of years ago; under God's Providence prodigy grew! It is still being expanded and improved. Throughout the world it is managed by politicians, often to its detriment. We hope things will improve! Many of the Sun's rays are quite well known, but there are more yet to be discovered. One that is likely to be discovered is one which is closely associated with life itself. Life has neither weight nor dimension, but it is present as life, drawing energy from the sun. It is present everywhere with its associated electricity; the two are one. More knowledge would increase understanding and link up with Providence. Man is falling short of possibilities. Life is becoming cheap!

The universe was constructed and is maintained using a

proved mathematical law, known and used with confidence worldwide!

The resourcefulness of life to accomplish a great purpose manifests a Creator of masterful intelligence and providential care for the whole of his creation.

Animal instinct shows the goodness to otherwise helpless creatures, of our Almighty God Creator.

The power of reason and imagination, greater than instinct, shows the infinite wisdom imbued in mankind by a loving God! Providential Care!

The economy of nature in face of man's wastefulness should be a great corrector! Can man see beyond his nose? The heavens declare the glory of God, and the firmament showeth his handiwork!!

Fundamentals and Prodigy

Movements in the universe: Distances are so great that to record them requires the lapse of lengthy periods. It is difficult to derive real information from the orderly state of the stars, which we observe in suitable conditions.

Our short life is right out of phase with time in the universe, and so we turn back to our solar system, where there is much food for thought, upon Providential Care!

Spiritual law in the universe: The control and maintenance in the universe are obviously under spiritual law. Orbits and cometology are complex and operationally perfect. The movements in the universe are positive, accurate, orderly, and completely effective as we observe them, but the universe is not an open book.

We can derive intense satisfaction in absolute faith in the God Creator.

Physical components are present on heavenly bodies and

are controlled by gravity and atmospheric pressure, fifteen pounds per square inch.

Atomic energy is produced and controlled in the universe.

An individual, by careful observation, can come to understand many things which illumine the mind, adding power of reckoning and reasoning. Control of the development of the mind is a function of the individual, selecting, gauging capacity, dimensions and content. Never allow this to be taken from you!

Think constructively of your entry into the universe at death. Providing you qualify, and this of course is essential: one thing you will require is a full manifestation of spiritual law!

This entirely depends on conscious development during lifetime on Earth! Such spiritual consciousness must be achieved on Earth, as it is the vehicle you must have to receive an indispensible item of knowledge in the hereafter. This to allow participation in that fuller life!

There are the common substances used in commerce and industry. These come from many sources. There are the chemical elements found in the earth, also those manufactured and mined. There is a complex of supply of coal of vegetable origin, as well as tin and copper, to mention just a few as an example of the providential creation for the use of God's creation. Many of these things lay ready for use for teeming millions of years, Do they go forever being used without a thought of where they came from?

There are the flowers and trees to beautify the Earth and cause a response in the mind, to smooth out the stresses of life and turn people into paths of thoughtfulness and contemplation. This can be a powerful influence towards lessening unrewarding selfishness.

Smallmindedness is common; it narrows concept and fixes smallness. Turn surely from these things to salute the great mind that instituted Providential Care, the Almighty Creator. He favours none but looks expectantly to everyone.

Four

Odes to Almighty God and His Worshipers, also Some Inanimates

ODE TO THE SUN

Sun, Sun, glorious Sun!
The Earth turns towards you, glorious Sun.
Sun, Sun, glorious Sun, by your power Day has begun.
Dawn approaches with promise of full light.
Bird song commences in chorus and banishes night.
Over the Earth warmth is now spreading.
People responding, their doubts are shedding.
Clouds sail over the brightening sky—
Darkening it might be, but hopes are high!
Flowers—the daisy opens to the sunlight.
All should be inspired by such a brave sight.
A dog barks its greeting in obvious joy.
Surely all should rejoice and respond in alloy.
The new day offers much in many opportunities.
All mankind should give welcome in unity.
What will the result be? Can we guess at it?
Better by far to respect than examine it.
More to the point would be to give it support!
Then it would be possible to claim a small part.
Such would be agreed in this land of the DART.

Written before breakfast at Buckfastliegh, where the sun shone each day of our holiday!

ODE TO THE SPRING

Spring, spring, brilliant spring,
Saluting us tunefully now the birds sing.
The trees produce beauteous tiny leaf.
Bushes in great variety are almost beyond belief.
The spring flowers are glorious in very rich colour.
The whole earth is dressed all this to follow.
The scheme is obviously to plume and present!
The object of creation is to increase consent.
Faced with prolific growth for a season,
Nature in full dress suggests a good reason.
It becomes important to look closely at it.
Some will deduce a commanding compliance.
Many will look, but place no reliance.
The mind must with insight be brought to bear.
The grand display happens once every year!
With the spring all should ponder anew!
The objective is clear; all should, to it, be true.
A warm spring day of glorious sunlight
Calls forth a response in thankful delight!
The Creator of all things makes a joyful provision.
Thoughtful observers will be mindful of virtue in vision.

ODE TO LIFE, TO BE LIVED, NOT MERE EXISTENCE

This life with duties and cares abounding
Houses difficulties, many quite astounding!
It can also bring much welcome relief
From very sore and heartfelt grief.
Life is life, not mere existence!
To live it well calls for continuous persistence.
Many there are who miss its quality fullness,
Because they bring to it disinterested dullness.
The great Creator's all-enveloping love
Strengthens those who strive for a life above!
There are rewards, which must be sought.
The Great God smiles upon a life well fought.
All can partake of this beneficence,
Even those who only start by contributing indifference.
The opportunities and satisfactions in creation's providence
Are freely available in clear-cut evidence.
They are not confined to those proven by goodness,
They are closely to hand in purposeful oneness!
There is reward for all who capably grow,
Much greater than man can easily know,
For God rewards every real endeavour
With an existence that goes on forever.
Truth, certainly not easy to define.
If tinctured by the resource of the spirit divine,
Can then be grasped and understood,
Thus made part of one's own aim, to establish brotherhood.
Many more fruits of real living are part of the purposes and
the very object of God's giving!
Do not allow this to escape your attention,
For this would result in loss too regrettable to mention!

ODE TO FRIENDSHIP (Moral)

Friendship illumines for us the great fundamentals of life!
It makes for happiness and never causes strife.
It is true to the very firm standards of conduct devised by man.
It would with horror abhor the departure from truth,
upholding right.
It gives stature to pleasantry with all its might.
It is never found wanting and always ready to help.
It knows not selfishness and so can forget self!
It is quickly to hand and very able to understand.
It is equipped to see duty and makes no demand.
It is its nature to give and has plenty in store.
It stands ready at all times able to offer more.
It is kind and considerate always, but never hides the truth.
It laughs and jokes but isn't ever uncouth!
There are times, indeed, when it can give only advice.
It stands by principle; to depart therefrom would not be nice.
It has spirit and scorns even thought of reward.
It listens with glee and smiles when that goes by a board!
It has life rich and fruitful; it will never be bold.
The value of friendship is a wealth of goodness untold.
In worth it is outstanding and cannot be bought.
It lives in the heart, where it grows, but cannot be taught.
It warms a cold heart from its inward strength.
When called upon, it responds, going to any length!
To boast, or talk of its actions it never would dream.
To it, such conduct a betrayal of confidence would seem.
Success makes for rejoicing, at each attainment in friendship's
name!

Unwarranted deception, disturbing disquieting, when overcome, achieves the same.
Difficulty dealt with and defeated brings quiet satisfaction and inward delight.
Often expensive in time, its object is clear in securing what is just and right.
Every phase and detail between friends is a sacred pledge of unity.
Such is the special nature of all acts in friendship's unanimity!

ODE TO MOTHERS

Mother dear, have you heard the song that is going round?
It is new and so very true that I kept my ear to the ground.
My Mother dear, it says very clear that you are loving and true.
I know, for all my life I have accorded you love that I never will rue.
There is wonder at and great respect for Mother's high regard!
Your children look up to you, for they see a strength that will never fail them.
You have always been to all children a source of sure and wonderful guidance.
Children come to you, knowing by your smiling welcome that they can trust you.
When they have doubts and fears, they straightaway wish to talk with you.
Children doing things without proper preparation seek a wise head to consult.
They are attracted by a light, which they see in your eye, Mother dear.
Children notice that which is part of what a mother has in her heart.
Children during their upbringing must be taught respect and its practice.
Children should be encouraged to seek out and study standard works.
Children should be made au fait with good manners in general.
Children quickly grow up and need a clear light to guide them towards duty.
Time passes and they must prepare to meet the need to accept leadership.
Children must not be found wanting when duty falls to their lot!
Children must be given a clear lead to recognize and accept responsibility.

Children must be given an appetite for sound and reliable thinking.

In this they must be shown the necessity for study and for careful reference.

Children will then respond and seek the means to show their interest.

Once started on a proper course, they are safely heading for maturity.

ODE TO REMEMBERING

Life is made of up of many routines and small occasions!
Much of this affords opportunities for thought and ovations.
The Creator has provided for happy pursuits and celebrations.
There are manifold possibilities for the mind, requiring preparation.
Foremost is the need for education and multi-channeled it has become.
Time, a factor predominant from birth, is uppermost in the years to come.
Decision is ever present, education should be for life and living.
To short-circuit it with a lesser role is a crime unforgivable.
There is little common ground, but thought should range wide and high.
Rejection will figure in these considerations; it will be ever nigh!
Hegel's logic, the philosopher's mind, these have a bearing.
The Christian ethic, unequaled in the world's religions, will heavily bear.
However, in this treatise, we will comment upon the present day!
Much has been said and written on the subject of education.
Advocacy has left little unsaid; we are concerned with the position today.
Human conduct deteriorates; standards thereof disappear in degeneration!
Facts are taught ad nauseam; indiscipline and noise are out of relation.
Education requires adjustment thankfulness and gratitude to God must be re-established in simplicity of acknowledgement.
Every moment of every day, every second that ticks away,
Father of all, to thee we say, Creator spirit, hear us pray!

What to thee should we pray? Words do not adequately frame our thought.
Our minds are full of gratitude; our hearts glow with thanks.
Our strength all flows from thee; our spirit is of thine own!
Our love is frail and cannot compare. Thy love is our life's greatest comfort.
Thy love cannot be bought; with full hearts our prayer is for guidance!
Thanks reflect our gratitude. Thy providential care bears on our whole life.
Thus from birth to death, we are conscious of thy greatness and in thy presence we know thine ineffable love!

ODE TO A PERFECT WIFE

The following is written after thirty-five years of wonderful happiness terminated by a fatal illness. The next twenty years to date will be sweetened by thoughts producing unforgettable memories!

The lovely charm of your manner and the perfect grace of all
your actions.
The love of your own folk and the care of those you held dear.
The giving, which was free and above your physical strength.
The charity in which you beheld others and the many
reflections of goodness as you interpreted living.
The noble purpose that you read into life and the wonderful
mastery of your knowlege of God!
The glorious certainty of your spirit and the faith, which you
daily demonstrated.
The understanding of life's difficulties and the tranquil peace
of your thoughts.
The exquisite beauty of your life and the firm grip of your
belief!
The vision of better things to come and the certainty of a life
hereafter.
The cheerful acceptance of God's will for you!

The foregoing are always uppermost in my thoughts of my wife and are a comfort to me. Each day I find new evidence of loving thought in things left behind for my good. Our life together suggests what I feel heaven must be like, and a meeting there in a new life is the most attractive thing that I can imagine and hope for!

I have ideas out of my observation of the beauty of the Earth, sea, and sky—of the possibilities the Creator could provide in another part of the universe. Further to this, the power in the stars we can observe is far greater than anything we know—tremendous sources of energy exist. Our sun is as a candlelight to some of the seats of power in the Milky Way and in other galaxies of innumerable stars indistinguishable to the naked eye. They are so distant in the universe.

Obviously the spiritual laws of the universe provide the only means of communication, as nothing physical, as we know it, could cross the tremendous distances involved. Many of the stars are suns much more powerful than our sun. The solar systems, which undoubtably exist, have not yet been discovered. They are isolated by great distance. Only the suns that control and power them can be seen.

ODE TO GOD—CREATOR

The Almighty God, Creator of Eternal Providential Care!
Based on ineffable love to demonstrate the magnanimity of all Creation.
Providential Care broadcast over all Creation without discrimination!
This a great objective from the heart and mind of the Almighty,
Who has, from the beginning, coordinated all forces, *His* aims to declare!
Spiritual law, a mighty force controlled by its Maker; basic in all movement in the universe!
These great forces in the universe, observable by all beings great and small.
The tremendous distances necessitating an accuracy, staggering to contemplate.
A measure of understanding being possible, by competent ability observing from Earth,
There being much to be aware of, which can inform and so stimulate zeal,
The stars in their courses giving man a practical demonstration of order.
New knowledge is needed to "Father" man's thoughtfulness in those directions!
Man to be actuated, urged into action in new fields, his life enhanced,
Appreciating the importance of improving "relations," achieving better understanding.
He must then make progress by wider designs near to God's purposes,
Making a contribution in the spirit, care, and concern, of his Maker, in all things,
Treading in the steps of the old Prophets, according with Christ's teaching.

Why is man so tardy his God Creator to understand?
Man must awaken to a better knowledge of the ordinance of God.
These actions of God, a positive permanence, man has a "God-given" capacity to understand.
God's providential care, a blessing that operates from birth to death and after for all believers.
The scope of this blessing is such that it operates, being present, in every eventuality in life!
An example is our solar system, which was designed and brought into existence by a great creative intelligence, using our known unalterable mathematical law.

The whole universe likewise! Especially is the distance of Earth from the Sun to obtain the conditions for the creation of all life, in its varied forms, on Earth only, in the Solar System. The tilt of 23 degrees from Earth's axis gives us our seasons. Atmospheric pressure gives the universe gravity. Electric power, sparking in the atmosphere, gives electrolysis, which is basic in evolution and in the process of germination, the energizing of the cell. One of the sun's rays of radiant energy being studied, as for instance light and heat are propagated; another the cell, which is the unit-mass of living matter in animals!

Hundreds of such blessings exist and can be detailed.

There is before us the challenge of the world-wide rampant evil of the present day and man's responsibility for measures determinately put into operation to arrest its progress!!

ODE TO SUNDOWN

Reflected light brilliant but not lasting!
Colour in great variety, much beyond asking,
Thought invoked, both warm and rewarding,
Repeated displays always awarded a welcome!
Memories awaken and enliven keen feeling,
Pleasures recalled and affirmed with alacrity!
Past, present, and future blending in ecstasy!
Tangible and very real are the hopes arising,
Inspired and resolute are the actions envisaged!
Visions of great possibilities occupy the mind,
Determined and resolute are the actions resulting,
Started by departing light in the calm of evening,
Made real by the wonderful display of colour!
Great are the results in refreshing experience,
Empowered and eager to proceed to sharing!!
Searching to found the ground for so doing,
Believing in the certainty of a kindred spirit!
Not be put off by the difficulty of communicating,
Encouraged by the evidence of real fellow feeling,
Acknowledging the soundness of the messages designed.
And displayed by nature, at sundown,
Activated under God by the splitting of the spectrum.